Uncharted, Unexplored, and Unexplained

Scientific Advancements of the 19th Century

Gregor Mendel
and the
Discovery of the Gene

Mitchell Lane
PUBLISHERS

P.O. Box 196
Hockessin, Delaware
19707

Uncharted, Unexplored, and Unexplained

Scientific Advancements of the 19th Century

Visit us on the web: www.mitchelllane.com
Comments? email us: mitchelllane@mitchelllane.com

Scientific Advancements of the 19th Century

Gregor Mendel
and the
Discovery of the Gene

by John Bankston

Uncharted, Unexplored, and Unexplained

Scientific Advancements of the 19th Century

Mitchell Lane
PUBLISHERS

Printing   1   2   3   4   5   6   7   8
    Library of Congress Cataloging-in-Publication Data
Bankston, John, 1974-
    Gregor Mendel and the discovery of the gene / John Bankston.
    p. cm. — (Uncharted, unexplored & unexplained: scientific advancements of the 19th century)
Includes bibliographical references and index.
    Contents: Giving peas a chance — Buying the farm —The order — Who are you — To the future.
    ISBN 1-58415-266-4 (lib. bdg.)
    1. Mendel, Gregor, 1822-1884 — Juvenile literature. 2. Geneticists—Austria—Biography—Juvenile literature. [1. Mendel, Gregor, 1822-1884. 2. Geneticists. 3. Scientists.] I. Title. II. Uncharted, unexplored & unexplained.
    QH31.M45B36 2005
    576.5'2'092--dc22   2003024134

ABOUT THE AUTHOR: ABOUT THE AUTHOR: Born in Boston, Massachusetts, John Bankston has written over three dozen biographies for young adults profiling scientists like Jonas Salk and Alexander Fleming, celebrities like Mandy Moore and Alicia Keys, great achievers like Alfred Nobel, and master musicians like Mozart. An avid reader and writer, he has had a lifelong love of science and music. He worked in Los Angeles, California as a producer, screenwriter and actor. Currrently he is in preproduction on *Dancing at the Edge*, a semi-autobiographical film he hopes to film in Portland, Oregon. Last year he completed his first young adult novel, *18 to Look Younger*.

PHOTO CREDITS: Cover: James King-Holmes/Science Photo Library; pp.6, 26 Hulton/Archive; p. 12 Mendelianum Morazké Zemské Muzeum; pp. 20, 28, 30, 34, 38, 39 Science Photo Library; p. 38 Corbis.

PUBLISHER'S NOTE: This story is based on the author's extensive research, which he believes to be accurate. Documentation of such research is contained on page 47.

The internet sites referenced herein were active as of the publication date. Due to the fleeting nature of some web sites, we cannot guarantee they will all be active when you are reading this book.

Uncharted, Unexplored, and Unexplained

Scientific Advancements of the 19th Century

Gregor Mendel

and the Discovery of the Gene

*For Your Information

As a young man, Gregor Mendel was always curious. He was always asking the kinds of questions that no one else had been able to answer to his satisfaction.

1

Giving Peas a Chance

The mice were starting to stink. Housed in a tiny cage in Gregor Mendel's room, the tiny creatures had a funk all their own. They weren't pets. They were part of an experiment that Gregor was conducting. He hoped to find out what happened when a white-haired mouse and a black-haired mouse had offspring. Would their fur be a blend of the two, producing gray-haired mice? Or would they be all white, or all black? What about the mice several generations later, what about the grand-children? What color would their fur be? Could one color disappear for a few generations and then reappear?

The year was 1854. Gregor was curious. As far as he was concerned, he was asking the kinds of questions that no one else had been able to answer to his satisfaction. This curiosity wasn't anything new. Gregor had always been curious, he was always asking questions. At the St. Thomas monastery near Brünn (today it is known as Brno, pronouned Burr-no), the capital of Moravia (part of the modern-day Czech Republic, though in those days it was a country in the sprawling Austro-Hungarian empire), he was in good company. The brotherhood of monks of which he was a member was well known for their scientific and literary pursuits as well as their religious studies. Unfortunately, not everyone shared their curiosity. When Bishop Anton Ernst Schaffgotsch visited Gregor's room, he was flabbergasted. Besides the foul odor, the Bishop didn't believe that breeding experiments were an appropriate pastime for a monk. He demanded that Gregor get rid of the mice at once.

Gregor was devastated. He probably should have seen it coming. The elderly bishop had been a constant source of annoyance to the monks of St. Thomas. He was a very conservative man who disapproved of many of the things they studied. In his opinion, the monastery seemed more like a college or university than a place of worship. The monks had taken a vow of chastity, which means that they would never have sex. In the bishop's opinion, it was highly inappropriate for Gregor to encourage sexual activity among the mice. Even worse, he would often watch it.

As if that wasn't enough, the bishop had a long memory. When he visited the monastery several years earlier, Gregor had whispered to another monk that Schaffgotsch had "more fat than understanding."[1] But Gregor hadn't been quiet enough. The bishop overheard him and was offended. There was no way that he would cut Gregor any slack now.

Despite the loss of his mice, Gregor refused to abandon his experiments. This wasn't the first time that he'd run into an obstacle. He'd come up against them all his life, from his farmer father who didn't understand why his boy wanted to go to college to a history of failing important tests. His unceasing curiosity kept him going.

Some bishop wasn't going to change that. Even though he disliked the bishop, Gregor had to obey his order. He got rid of the mice but quickly found a substitute: peas. Rodents and vegetables might not seem to have much in common. Gregor knew differently.

"I turned from animal breeding to plant breeding," Gregor later said with a chuckle. 'You see, the bishop did not understand that plants also have sex."[2]

Just like animals, the result of "plant sex" was offspring. The "parents" passed on their traits—such as color, texture, size, and so forth—

to the next generation. It was these traits that Gregor wanted to know about. Peas, mice, people and every living thing on earth have a collection of traits that are passed down. It's why a baby might have her mother's eyes, her father's nose and a great aunt's chin.

While it wasn't his intention, the order that the bishop issued almost certainly worked out better for Gregor. His room smelled a lot better after the mice were removed. In addition, dealing with peas took advantage of Gregor's upbringing. He had grown up on a farm, where he'd watched his father cross breed fruit trees. His father would insert a shoot from one plant into another, then allow them to grow together and form a single plant. This process was called grafting. In addition to this practical experience, Gregor was skilled in math. Using numbers to organize his pea experiments and determine various traits, Gregor was one of the first to practice the science of what we now call genetics.

Yet he wasn't even a scientist. He was an obscure monk living in poverty. His work was tedious and demanding. Although he published

Pea plants provided Gregor with the same opportunity for experimentation as did the mice. The bishop did not understand that plants also have sex.

several papers describing his research, few people read them. Gregor was ahead of his time. His fame would not arrive until he was long dead. That was something he predicted while he was still a teenager.

"The highest goal of earthly ecstasy;" he wrote, "that of seeing, when I arise from the tomb; my art thriving peacefully, among those who are to come after me."[3]

Although Gregor didn't live long enough to see his work recognized, his experiments put him on the same level with the most celebrated scientists of all time. His research in the nineteenth century paved the way for the amazing scientific realities of the twenty-first, from cloning to predicting diseases before babies are even born. Gregor Mendel was a monk ahead of his time. This is his story.

Monasteries are often more than ancient buildings where monks pray and study religion. Prior to Johann Gutenberg's invention of moveable type in the 1400s, monks were responsible for transcribing books by hand. A number of monastery collections still have these beautiful books that reveal their painstaking calligraphy. Many monasteries, like St. Thomas, also became important centers of learning where men who didn't have to worry about earning a living studied arts and sciences.

Josef Stalin

Founded in the fourteenth century, the St. Thomas monastery was located in the center of Brünn for several centuries. In the late 1700s, Emperor Josef II, who was upset with the Catholic Church, abolished many monasteries. St. Thomas was more fortunate, though the monks of St. Thomas were forced to relocate to the outskirts of the town. Many of their resources went towards repairing the ruined building they moved into.

Despite the building's flaws, the monks made sure the library was top-notch. The floor made of glistening hardwood. Everyone had to put on wool slippers before entering to protect its highly polished finish. Twenty thousand books lined the shelves on three sides of the room. Huge windows on the fourth side admitted light and offered views of the orchard. A false bookcase opened from one of the walls, revealing a door and five steps to a study area below where the monks could work and study in privacy.

St Thomas' Church is seen at the top left of the photo.

Sadly, part of the collection of St. Thomas was destroyed in the 1950s. By then Czechoslovakia was under the control of the Soviet Union and its communist leader Josef Stalin. Stalin was opposed to the church and to the theories of Gregor Mendel. He believed that under communism, people, plants and animals could be turned into anything that the government wanted them to be regardless of their heredity. Fortunately, many of Mendel's private papers were rescued.

This famous photograph is of members of the Augustianian monastery in Brno in the early 1860's. Gregor Mendel is standing, second in from the right.

2

Buying the Farm

Anton Mendel worked hard. He labored in silence, hoping he'd be able to provide a better life for his family. Just owning his own house was a step in the right direction, but in the 1830s he was still working part time for someone else. Three days a week he left his own small farm and worked on the much larger farm owned by his landlord, Countess Walpurga Truchess-Zeil. These farms were near the town of Heinzendorf. It was located in the northeast corner of Moravia, which at that time was part of the Hapsburg empire. One of the most powerful and richest families in Europe, the Hapsburgs had benefited from the feudal system for many centuries. Now the system was in its final stages. Anton's efforts allowed him to eventually own his farm.

Life was a struggle. It didn't get easier when Anton and his wife Rosine had a son on July 22, 1822. They named him Johann, which means "full of hope." His parents surely hoped for the day when their boy could help his father on the farm.

It wasn't to be. Although Johann would be the couple's only boy—his sister Veronica was two years older, Theresia would arrive when he was seven—he didn't want to work on a farm. His talents were mental, not physical.

13

The Countess provided classrooms and teachers for the children of all the people who worked for her. Unfortunately many of the lessons did little more than prepare them to be farmers. Most landowners didn't even provide a limited education. Johann was lucky to be able to go to school at all. Yet from his first year, he was ahead of everyone. He quickly lived up to the school motto, "money and property can be taken from me but never the art of scientific knowledge."[1]

Johann would always have trouble with money and property, but the part about scientific knowledge came easily. By the time he was eleven years old, he'd impressed his teacher Thomas Makitta so much that the man paid a special visit to the boy's parents. He explained that there was a better school for their son in Leipnik. It was thirteen miles away, far enough in the 1830s that Johann would have to live there. He didn't mind. Any nervousness about missing his home was buried by his desire for a challenge. After his teacher left, Johann begged his parents to let him go to the school.

Anton thought it was a bad idea. He needed his son's help on the farm. Besides, the family couldn't afford it. Rosine won the day, convincing her husband that only a top education would give their child the opportunities they'd never had.

Anton relented.

Johann rewarded their faith in him by excelling at his new school. By the end of the term, he was ranked at the top of the class. Now he had a new opportunity. The school he was attending was like a middle school. At twelve years of age, he was qualified to transfer to the Imperial Royal Gymnasium in Opava, an advanced high school designed to prepare its students for a university education. Although this would be quite an achievement, his already strapped parents could barely afford the expense. Johann was put on half rations, which meant that he only got half the food the other students received. His parents were expected to make up the rest. Although his mother sent him bread and vegetables (Johann really loved cucumbers) he often went hungry.

Things got even worse. Writing about himself, Johann would later recall that "During 1838, as the outcome of a rapid succession of mishaps, his parents were rendered unable to pay his school expenses, and the scholar, then sixteen years of age, was unfortunately compelled to fend for himself."[2]

The young man might not have made it, except once again his teachers saw his gift. Johann wasn't just a talented student. He was a talented teacher. They noticed how he explained lessons to his fellow students, the way he understood certain scientific principles much more quickly than his peers. Johann took an examination and was soon qualified to be a tutor. The job paid enough to cover his expenses.

Life soon had another test for Johann. That winter, his father was cutting down trees when one collapsed onto him. He was badly hurt. For the rest of the season he did little but try to recover. He was the sole provider for the family.

Johann stayed in school.

By May, Anton was working again. The hard labor of his life was worsened by his injuries, but he didn't have a choice. His family would starve if he didn't work. When Johann came home for the summer holidays, Anton must have hoped the teenager would take some of the load from his sagging shoulders.

Instead, Johann went quickly to his room. The next day he didn't leave, nor the next. His father grumbled but he was too confused by his son's mysterious illness, too weak from his injuries to do anything.

Johann retreated from the family, remaining in his room, sleeping late in a household used to rising with the dawn. His older sister ignored him. His younger sister was scared and unable to do anything. Only his mother took care of him, bringing his meals, and convinced her young scholar was at death's door.

He wasn't. Over a century later, Johann might have been diagnosed with depression, a mental illness that often immobilizes its sufferers if it is left untreated. Of course, when Johann was alive, there wasn't a treatment for depression other than time.

Time worked its cure when the fall term came. Johann returned to school, tutoring until his graduation in 1840. He needed to take a two-year course in the history of philosophy, along with advanced mathematics, before he could hope to be admitted to a university. The closest institute where he could take those courses was the University Philosophical Institute of Olmütz. It was in a town where Czech was the primary language and the German-speaking Johann had a hard time communicating. His Czech was poor so he wasn't much use as a tutor. Once again his lack of money drove him into darkness, as depression washed over him like a gray fog. His grades declined along with his optimism.

"The gloomy outlook upon the future, had so marked an effect upon him that he fell sick," Johann again wrote about himself, "and was compelled to spend a year with his parents for the restoration of his health."[3]

Having not finished a semester, he returned to the farm and the sanctuary of his bedroom. The pressure to help out never diminished, but he didn't seem to be able to do anything except think and feel bad. His sadness was relieved in 1841, when both of his sisters saved him.

First, Veronica got married. Her husband, Alois Sturm, bought the farm, paying Anton for his meager estate. The brother-in-law's money provided a way back to school.

Theresia had received a share of the sale, which was supposed to go towards her dowry. This was money a woman in the nineteenth century was expected to give to her husband as a wedding present when she got married. Maybe Theresia was too young to think much about getting married. Maybe she just wanted Johann's room.

Regardless, the young girl gave Johann her money so he could afford school. He promised her that he'd pay her back somehow, some way.

That time would not come for many years.

Instead he struggled for two years at the Philosophical Institute, trying to survive on his sister's loan, scholarship money and whatever little tutoring income he received. It still wasn't enough. No matter how hard he struggled, Johann was always broke. Failure was becoming familiar.

Once again a teacher saved him. Johann's physics professor, Friedrich Franz, was also a Catholic priest. He told Johann about a monastery, a place where his education would be paid for and he'd be able to live in an environment devoted to study. For many young men, taking a lifetime vow of poverty and chastity would have been too high a price. For Johann, it didn't look like he'd be giving up much.

In this map of Europe you can locate Brno in the Czech Republic.

Imagine working on land you don't really own, and giving part of your income to the landlord. You're committed to military service, and you have few rights. In fact, this landlord can act as a judge and have you punished if you're accused of a crime.

It wasn't slavery, but it was pretty close. As Anton Mendel tilled his farm, he was slowly exiting from a system that had endured for over one thousand years.

It was called the feudal system, or feudalism. It began during the eighth and ninth centuries. In structure, it resembled a pyramid. At the very top was a member of royalty, such as a king or queen. Directly under the royalty were important noblemen, such as barons, dukes and earls. Each of these noblemen had a number of minor nobles, or vassals, who served them. The base of the pyramid consisted of a huge population of peasants, or serfs as they were also known. The king or queen rewarded the nobility with enormous tracts of prime farmland. In exchange, they pledged the men who worked the land to serve in the royal army.

Life was hard for the peasants. They worked long hours in the fields and had to give much of what they grew to their masters. Their homes were small, usually just one or two rooms, and often drafty and cold. The one consolation was that in general they were safer under the feudal system than they would have been if they were living on their own.

Emperor Charles I of Austria (1887-1922) the last of the Habsburg emperors. Shown with his wife, Empress Zita and their children.

As towns grew and became more important, the feudal system began to decline. By the mid-1800s, revolutions across Europe eliminated feudalism altogether. Eventually many laborers like Anton Mendel were able to own their own land.

This is the experimental garden where Mendel studied pea plants. It is located at the Abbey of Saint Thomas, Brno in the Czech Republic.

3

The Order

Johann Mendel was a "young man of very solid character,"[1] Father Franz wrote to Abbot Cyrill Napp of the St. Thomas monastery. He was "almost the best"[2] in his physics class, Franz added. While this may have not been the best recommendation in the world, it was enough to get Johann accepted into the Augustinian order of the St. Thomas Monastery. There were many other applicants but Johann was the only one that Franz thought was qualified.

He joined the order on October 9, 1843. As was customary, he immediately gave himself a new name to symbolize his new life: Gregor.

Named after St. Augustine, a great lover of books and knowledge who lived from the mid-fourth to the mid-fifth century, the Augustinians were probably the most laid back of the Catholic orders. They lived under relatively few rules and strictures compared to the Benedictines, the Franciscans and others who still took vows of silence, or spent their entire days in prayer. Instead the monks at St. Thomas were encouraged to study science and the arts, following the saint after whom their order was named. St. Augustine believed that prayers allowed people to talk to God, while reading allowed God to talk to them.

There was another advantage. Monks in the other orders often lived in tiny, sparsely furnished rooms that were little more than cubicles. At St. Thomas, Gregor and the others enjoyed well-furnished two-room apartments.

The former Johann, now Gregor, probably felt like he could truly breathe for the first time in his life. He didn't have to worry about money, about housing, and most of all he didn't have to worry about where his next meal was coming from. The cooks at the monastery were so talented that chefs traveled long distances just to study with them. The meals were elaborate and regular and Gregor rarely missed one. He soon became a very fat, and much more jolly, young man.

Abbot Napp took a special interest in him. Now in his late fifties, the abbot loved botany, the science that deals with plants. Once he realized that Gregor had grown up on a farm, he figured the new monk might have a natural gift for botany. He sent Gregor to the Brünn Theological College, where Gregor quickly proved that the abbot was right.

At the school he excelled in more than just religious studies. He was the prize pupil of Franz Diebl, the school's professor of agriculture. For the first time, Gregor began to understand the science behind his father's work cross breeding fruit trees.

Of course, Gregor understood only part of the science. Much of what causes plants and other living creatures to pass on various qualities to their offspring was unknown when he was in school.

In fact, Gregor would be the one who would solve many of those puzzles.

Diebl explained that there was a reason why plants "bred true." This was when hybrids of the same type were bred to pass on their qualities to offspring, creating potentially brand new species. Gregor absorbed all he could, realizing that this was a subject which would interest him long after the course was over. He began to design breeding experiments, collecting mice to see what would happen when a black-haired mouse and a white-haired mouse mated.

There was just one problem with Gregor's new life in the monastery. As part of his duties, Gregor was expected to visit St. Anne's Hospital and minister to the sick. This was not exactly an ideal job for him. Being around the ill and dying made the already sensitive young man so depressed that he almost fell into his old pattern. Fortunately the abbot quickly realized the problem. He temporarily released Gregor from those duties and put him to work in the greenhouse.

It was a perfect fit. All his life Gregor would suffer from chills. That was a real burden in Brünn, which could become very cold. The monastery was drafty even in summer. But beneath the glass of the greenhouse, Gregor could soak in the sun. Laboring alone with the plants, a job that many people might find tedious, was restful for him.

Perhaps Gregor's fear of going to St. Anne's saved his life. For while he battled mental illness, in 1847 physical illness was taking its toll on the monks of St. Thomas. Three priests died of diseases they may have caught while working in St. Anne's. Because of the loss, the monastery was short-handed. Gregor and several others who'd joined at the same time as he did were rushed through the steps toward becoming a priest. In less than four years, he went from novice to sub-deacon, deacon and priest. He was ordained in the summer of 1847, soon after he reached the minimum age for a priest of twenty-five.

By all accounts, Gregor's parents were proud of their son. In the nineteenth century, there was no greater honor for most Catholic families than having a son who succeeded in becoming a member of the priesthood. Unfortunately his new-found status forced him to return to the hospital. Besides the emotional toll, every hour that he was there kept him away from his scientific studies.

A new year brought a new depression as Gregor retreated into his cell during the early weeks of January. Coming so soon after the other deaths, the members of St. Thomas surely worried that Gregor's illness was physical, and made sure he wasn't dying. When the abbot realized that the sickness was in response to Gregor's work at the hospital, he didn't get upset. Instead, he found something better for him.

"He is very diligent in the study of the sciences," the abbot wrote in a letter to the bishop, "much less fitted for work as a parish priest, the reason being that he is seized by an unconscious timidity when he has to visit a sick bed or to see anyone ill or in pain. Indeed, this infirmity of his has made him dangerously ill."[3]

Bishop Schaffgotsch never forgot Gregor's joke about his weight (truly in poor taste considering Gregor's own girth) but he was under orders from the government. Priests had to be more involved in their communities, especially as teachers.

Beginning in the fall of 1849, Gregor Mendel was rescued from the hospitals and the shelter of his cell. He began teaching math and classics at a school in a nearby town. He didn't have a college degree or a teacher's certificate, but most of the students loved the portly priest who brought the same enthusiasm to teaching that he'd brought to the greenhouse.

Years later one of his former students would remember, "We all loved Mendel. I recall his dear, loyal face, his kindly eyes which often had a roguish twinkle, his fair, curly head, his rather squat figure, his upright gait, the way he always looked straight up in front of him."[4]

By 1850, Gregor Mendel's life was very busy. He was teaching twenty hours a week, reading and grading papers in Latin, Greek and mathematics. At the monastery he labored in his greenhouse and attended religious services. In the little free time he had, Gregor tried to prepare for his upcoming teacher examination. Then, as now, teachers needed to be certified in order to teach. For Gregor this meant writing essays dealing with current science and answering the questions of examiners.

Gregor did poorly in both. For the first part of his two-part examination, Gregor relied on outdated and often incorrect information in answering his test questions. While his monastery libraries probably had advanced scientific texts, for some reason Gregor didn't seem to want to use them. The result was he only passed half of the exam. Still, he had another chance to redeem himself.

The second part of the test found him traveling to Vienna. He arrived in the middle of August. Unfortunately, a letter telling him that the test had been rescheduled didn't reach him in time. The examiners had been planning on leaving on a summer holiday. Instead they were forced to stay in the sweltering city and test the poorly prepared monk. They were not happy.

Suddenly overcome by nerves, Gregor seemed to offer the first idea that came to mind. In the question on zoology he actually wrote, "The cat is a useful animal because it exterminates [kills] mice."[5] His answers to the examiner's questions were just as bad.

Afterward, one of the examiners wrote in his evaluation, "The part of the question which relates to the utility of animals... is answered in the most schoolboy fashion."[6] Worse, the grader concluded with, "This written examination paper would hardly allow us to regard him as competent to become an instructor even at a lower school."[7]

Gregor was sure he was finished. He returned to the monastery feeling utterly defeated. The security of his room was calling. He might well have slipped into another depressive episode. Once again Abbot Napp came to the rescue.

He realized that the twenty-eight year old monk's failure wasn't his fault. After all, he'd failed an exam normally given to college graduates. So the answer was simple. The monastery would send Gregor to college.

"Father Gregor Mendel has proven unsuitable for work as a parish priest," Abbot Napp admitted in his letter of recommendation to the University of Vienna, "but has on the other hand shown evidence of exceptional intellectual capacity and remarkable industry in the study of the natural sciences...for the full practical development of his powers in this respect it would seem necessary and desirable to send him to Vienna, where he will have full opportunities to study."[8]

Gregor arrived late, a familiar pattern for him. It was October, classes were in full swing and he was dreadfully far behind.

While at the University of Vienna, he was able to take courses and began to focus on mathematics. Founded in 1365 by Duke Rudolph IV, the school had an impressive reputation (and would later produce several Nobel Prize winners). It was an excellent time for Gregor to attend. He studied botany with a man who was tops in the field, Franz Unger, and physics with Christian Doppler, whose sound wave theory would make him famous.

This photo is of the University of Vienna where Mendel took courses and began to focus on math.

Gregor returned to Brünn in 1853. The following year he got another teaching job, this time at a high school not far from the monastery. In 1856, he took another test for his teacher's certificate. Again he failed. Nevertheless, he would teach at the same school for twelve more years although he didn't earn the same amount of money that he would if he had been certificated.

Failing the test again hardly seemed to matter. By that time his interests were starting to expand. In the garden of the monastery, he was beginning to experiment with heredity, while in England a naturalist named Charles Darwin was about to astonish the world with his own theories.

Charles Darwin

*Charles Darwin was an English naturalist who
spent five years on the sailing vessel Beagle on an
around-the-world cruise between 1831 and 1836. He
spent much of that time on shore, collecting specimens
and observing plants and animals. He devoted more
than twenty years evaluating his findings after he
returned. Darwin published these findings in* On the
Origin of Species *in 1859. It sold out its first printing in
a day and made its author world famous.*

*Darwin's theory held that complex organisms evolve,
or change, through a series of small steps. These steps occur due to random
changes in genetic instructions.*

*The giraffe's long neck serves as an example of evolution. Over a period of
thousands of years, short-necked giraffes might give birth to giraffes with
slightly longer necks, which is called a mutation. These "mutants" would be
able to eat leaves that grow higher on trees, leaves that were unavailable to the
giraffes with shorter necks. Because they were able to eat better, these "mutant"
giraffes would have a better chance of survival. In turn, they would produce
mutant offspring with even longer necks. Eventually giraffe necks reached the
size with which we are familiar today. Darwin gave the term "natural selection"
to this process.*

*Gregor devoured the book when it became available in a German translation
and made extensive notes in the margins. For him, it was an example of a
curious mind making progress in a field where better-educated scientists had
failed. He agreed with many of Darwin's ideas. But he had one area of disagree-
ment. Darwin believed in the idea of blending inheritance. Just as we can mix
blue and yellow paints to produce green, he felt that offspring would combine
parents' characteristics in a new way. Gregor believed otherwise. His theory of
dominant and recessive traits would have helped Darwin better explain how
natural selection works.*

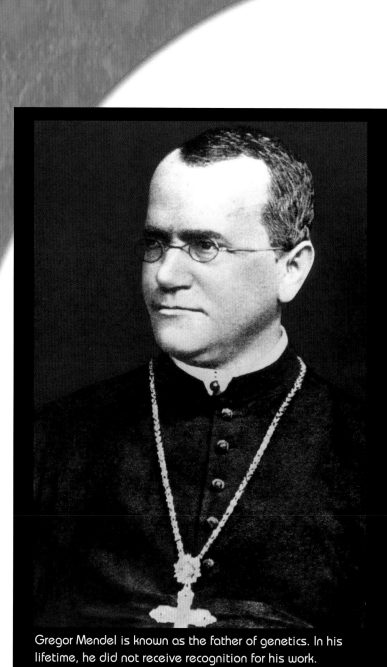

Gregor Mendel is known as the father of genetics. In his lifetime, he did not receive recognition for his work.

4

Who You Are

For as long as people have noticed a similarity between their own faces and a distant relative's, the question of heredity has been a mystery. Why do we look the way we do? Why do heart disease and mental illness and a thousand other things seem to run in families?

By Gregor's time, the question of how we become who we are had been explored for over two thousand years. The man considered to be the father of medicine, Hippocrates, theorized in about 400 B.C. that tiny particles from a man's body could be found in his semen. These combined with female fluid during breeding. Because the particles were drawn from throughout the man's entire body, his offspring resembled him. This theory was known as pangenesis.

Not long afterward, the theory of pangenesis was disputed by a fellow Greek, the philosopher Aristotle. Aristotle believed that offspring took on the characteristics of both parents. He also believed of the two parents, the male was likely to pass on more traits than the female. According to Aristotle, these traits were passed on through the blood of the parents, which is probably where we get phrases such as "blood relatives," "bloodlines" and even "bluebloods," a term that refers to members of the aristocracy (Unlike peasants, they didn't spend much time in the sun. So when they turned their hands over and looked at their wrists, their blood vessels appeared blue against their pale skin).

Aristotle's theory persisted for many centuries. It wasn't until the invention of the microscope that scientists began to be able to offer better (but still wrong) explanations.

The Greek philosopher Aristotle believed that offspring took on the characteristics of both parents. He believed that these traits passed on through the blood of the parents. His theories continued for many centuries until scientists were able to offer better explanations.

In the 1600s, Dutch scientist Anton van Leeuwenhoek was convinced he was watching a tiny baby form when he merged semen with embryonic fluid and looked at it through a microscope. In 1665, Robert Hooke first gave the name of "cells" to the tiny organisms he could see through the lens of a microscope. He thought they looked like the little cells, or rooms, where monks lived.

Less than two hundred years later, it would take an actual monk— Gregor—to examine the question of heredity, the question of how living things take on the qualities of relatives. As a result, modern genetics can be traced back to his work. And he didn't even use a microscope.

After his first experiments with mice were cut short by the bishop, Gregor turned to plants. He decided to focus on the pea. It was an ideal choice. There were many different kinds—short, tall, wrinkled, round, etc. The pea could cross-pollinate. The pollen went from one pea to another, producing new peas that were a combination of the two. It could also self-pollinate, producing more seedlings (and future peas) all by itself. Each generation of peas took far less time to develop than the mice. Gregor was able to get his questions answered in a fairly short period of time.

The work he embarked on was a perfect fit for his nature. It was quiet and solitary. It required a knowledge of science, and a physical ability to handle plants. Most importantly, it required mathematical precision—he would have to be able to express the chances that certain traits would appear as numbers. Only by predicting the future could he solve a riddle from the past.

Mendel made sure that his "laboratory," a garden near the monastery's library, was carefully controlled. He handled the pollination himself, cutting off the peas' anthers—the pollen-producing part of a plant—to prevent self-pollination. Then he covered the opened lower buds with tiny calico caps. A few days after he did this, he used a camel's hair brush to carefully sweep pollen from peas with intact anthers. The plants he "impregnated" were the ones he studied.

Gregor selected peas from a variety of pods—long and short, green and yellow—which came from two types of seeds: wrinkled and round. By cross pollinating, or transferring pollen from one plant to another, he was able to breed plants that "bred true" so a specific trait appeared. With each new generation, he noticed that a pea would often have qualities not seen in the pea it came from, traits that were present in earlier generations. Some plants grown from round seeds would have offspring that bore wrinkled seeds, some green pea pods produced yellow pea pods.

Mendel examined what he referred to as seven character traits, or the German word *merkmals*—something you could see. He also referred (less frequently) to *elementes* (another German word), things you cannot see. These *elementes*, he believed, were responsible for the *merkmals*. In other words, the unseen *elementes* made the character traits appear.

In the twentieth century a word for these *elementes* was first used: genes.

Gregor looked at seven characteristics: seed shape, seed color, tint, height, where the flowers are, along with the color and shape of the unripe pod. This work required complex mathematical formulas and precise "harvesting" of the peas. In fact from 1856- 1863 he examined 28,000 peas.

By 1863, he had his answer. Gregor came up with "heredity laws." Most would eventually be proven in the twentieth century, some nearly one hundred years after his experiments!

Gregor Mendel determined that each pea plant owned a pair of *elementes*. Each of them controlled a trait in the plant—whether it was yellow, green, long or short. Each *elemente* could either be strong or weak. The strong *elemente* is what we would now call a "dominant gene" and the weak *elemente* is now referred to as a "recessive gene."

In the laws he crafted, plants that inherited two strong traits—one from each parent—would have the strong trait. If the gene for a green plant was dominant, then its offspring would be green. If a plant inherited the strong gene and the weak gene, it would have the strong trait. Mendel noticed how these genes are inherited independently. The plant can inherit one gene without the other. This is why traits can appear which are not seen in the parents. It is why yellow pea pods can have offspring with green pods. It is also why some brown-eyed parents have blue-eyed children, even though the gene for blue eyes is recessive. The child probably has a blue-eyed grandparent.

By working with pea pods and mathematical precision, Gregor Mendel crafted a set of laws that would eventually be proven to be correct. His reward? Total obscurity.

The area of central Europe where Gregor Mendel lived suffered from almost constant division and redivision. Countries often seemed to change borders and rulers with the seasons. The region was once part of the Holy Roman Empire. After Napoleon Bonaparte's defeat at Waterloo in 1815, it recombined to form a loose allegiance of thirty-nine states known as the German Confederation. Many of these states did not get along.

Otto Von Bismarck

When Otto Von Bismarck became prime minister of the kingdom of Prussia in 1862, it quickly took a leading role in the German Confederation. In 1864, he led a brief war against Denmark. Following that conflict, he turned his attention to Austria, the other dominant member of the confederation.

In the summer of 1866, over 5,000 Prussian soldiers traveled through Brünn on their way to a battle with Austrian troops. The St. Thomas Monastery was in their path. Over one hundred soldiers stayed there, demanding shelter and food. After they left, a cholera epidemic swept through Brünn; the disease had arrived with the soldiers.

Prussia quickly and easily defeated Austria and formed the North German Confederation. Austria was reorganized as Austro-Hungary. Bismarck's final step was to provoke a war with France. The overwhelming German victory in 1871 led to the creation of a German empire with Prussia at the controls. It also led to fears of rising German power among the other major nations of Europe. Those fears would eventually lead to World War I, which lasted from 1914 to 1918. The harsh terms imposed on Germany after the war were one of the main causes of World War II, which cost millions of lives between 1939 and 1945. Soon afterward, the countries of central Europe came under the control of the Soviet Union. Two revolutions—Hungary in 1956 and Czechoslovakia in 1968—were put down violently. The Soviet Union collapsed in 1989 and the region has been at peace since then.

This is an oil painting of Gregor Mendel. In 1900, scientists rediscovered his work and saw that it was the basis of genetics.

5

To the Future

Gregor Mendel was nervous. It was 1865, and he was about to present his findings to the Brünn Society for the Study of Natural Science. Made up of scientists and laymen, the group gave locals with an interest in science a chance to discuss developments in their field. Appearing before them, Gregor felt like he was back in Vienna, trying to get his teaching certificate.

Except this time he knew most of the answers.

It didn't matter. The group seemed bored, and they didn't ask him very many questions. His presentation was reported in the group's magazine the following year, but the article gained him little respect and few readers. His theories on genetics were obscured by more trendy hypotheses. Few people understood how revolutionary his theories were.

In spite of the discouraging reception that his talk and his paper received, Gregor didn't give up. He did studies on hawkweed and eventually published a paper that detailed his research, although the results were not as startling as they'd been with the peas. He worked with other plants as well. These included beans, corns and several types of flowers. He kept up with the latest scientific research.

Eventually the disinterest in his work became Gregor's final defeat. He turned to monastery business. After the death of his mentor Abbot Napp in 1867, Gregor was elected to succeed him the following year. He also became chairman of the Moravian Mortgage Bank. In his later years, Gregor assumed a level of responsibility he couldn't have imagined when he was young.

He also assumed new and more expansive living quarters in the monastery, as well as an increase in his salary. He proved to be very generous with his money. He had never forgotten his younger sister's financial help when he needed additional funding for his own studies as a teenager. He repaid her generosity by paying for extensive schooling for her three sons. He also contributed to residents of Brünn who were in financial difficulties and helped them establish a fire station.

The Vatican can be seen in the distance in Rome, Italy.

His contributions weren't limited to money. He became a member of the Agricultural Society of Moravia. He wrote for the group's magazine and answered questions about the best ways of growing fruit trees.

His official duties as head of the monastery required frequent trips to inspect the properties it owned. He also had to make longer trips to the Vatican City in Rome to meet the Pope, as well as official visits to Vienna and Berlin.

It's not surprising that he didn't have much time left over. He conducted his final experiments with plants in 1871. Yet he retained his lifelong interest in science. Beginning in 1848, he had begun keeping records of the weather. He started publishing them in 1862 and eventually predicted that it would be possible to forecast the weather. The weather almost cost him his life one day in 1870. A freak tornado ripped through Brünn and hurled some roof tiles into his room. He also worked with bees, establishing a bee house in the monastery's garden and doing some research.

He even became involved in politics, though it wasn't entirely by choice. In 1875, the government established a new law that required monasteries to pay a heavy tax on their property. Gregor refused. He wrote angry letters to government officials and hoped for support from other people. There was none. Gradually he became more and more isolated.

"Gregor became suspicious of everyone, even his fellow monks, whom he thought to be 'nothing but enemies, traitors and intriguers,' writes Robin Marantz Henig. "In the end he could count on only three young men to stand by him: his nephews, the sons of his beloved sister Theresia."[1]

On January 6, 1884, Gregor died of kidney disease. The obituary in the *Tagesbote*, the local newspaper, said, "His death deprives the poor of a benefactor and mankind at large of a man of the noblest character, one who was a warm friend, a promoter of the natural sciences and an exemplary priest."[2]

There was no mention of his groundbreaking work in heredity. That is hardly surprising. When he died, few scientists even knew who he was. But Gregor Mendel's contribution to the natural sciences would eventually be understood.

Sixteen years later, a series of experiments by Hugo de Vries, Karl Correns and Erich Tschermak utilizing Mendel's papers proved that many of his theories were correct. The trio gave credit to the late scientist.

As the twentieth century progressed, the study of genetics gained respectability. In his book *What Mad Pursuit*, Francis Crick points out, "Genetics tells us that, roughly speaking we get half of all our genes from our mother, in the egg, and the other half from our father, in the sperm."[3] Since a single sperm is too small to be seen without a microscope, it stands to reason genes must be quite small as well. "Yet in this small space," explains Crick, "must be housed an almost complete set of instructions for building an entire human being (the egg providing the duplicate set.)."[4]

In 1905, an English biologist named William Bateson coined the term "genetics." It was based on the Greek word *genesis*, meaning "to give birth to." He introduced his new term at a conference the following year that dealt with plant breeding. The name of the conference was quickly changed to the International Genetics Congress. In 1909, Danish

This famous photograph shows James Watson (left) and Francis Crick (right) discussing their double helix DNA model. Crick and Watson were the first to map the basic structure of DNA.

researcher Wilhelm Johannsen used the same Greek root to come up with "gene" to describe the units of inheritance.

American scientist Thomas Hunt Morgan achieved a major advance in 1910. He chose fruit flies for his genetic experiments because a new generation could be produced every few days. That way he could see genetic changes very quickly. He confirmed Gregor's laws of heredity and established that genes were located on chromosomes.

Colored Scanning Electron Micrograph (SEM) of the fruit fly *Drosophila melanogaster* on a leaf. Drosophila melanogaster is widely used in genetic experiments because it reproduces very quickly and is easily manipulated in the laboratory.

The next step was determining what chromosomes were made of. For years, scientists believed that they were proteins, which seemed capable of containing great amounts of genetic information. In 1944, Oswald Avery proposed that deoxyribonucleic acid, or DNA, was responsible for carrying genetic information. He was ridiculed, but eight years later other experimenters proved that he was correct. In 1953, Francis Crick and James Watson mapped the basic structure of DNA. It enabled researchers to crack the genetic "code."

As Crick points out, "The general plan of living things seems almost obvious. Each gene determines a particular protein. Some of these proteins are used to form structures or carry signals, while many of them are the catalysts that decide what chemical reactions should and should not take place in each cell. Almost every cell in our bodies has a complete set of genes within it, and this chemical program directs how each cell metabolizes, grows and interacts with its neighbors."[5]

Technology also did its part to renew interest in Gregor's work. Microscopes became more powerful and the chromosomes that carried the genes could actually be viewed. It was possible for the first time to actually see much of what Mendel had determined mathematically.

It seems that every year brings new advances in genetics. DNA evidence is used in courtrooms to convict those guilty of crimes, and prove the innocence of others. Some animals have been cloned. More recently, several researchers have reported their ability to clone humans, although that is very controversial. The Human Genome Project, a cooperative international effort, seeks to identify the genetic makeup of every human chromosome. This project was completed in 2003.

In many ways these developments can be traced back to the garden of the St. Thomas Monastery, and the work of a single, somewhat troubled monk.

"Mendel might be embarrassed to see himself turned from a quiet, obscure, and brilliant man into the larger-than-life heroic figure he has become today," writes Janet Marantz Henig. "Mendel was a dogged worker, not a hero—and it was his nonheroism that allowed him to do the plodding, patient, thorough work through which his genius emerged."[6]

According to Francis Crick, there are three main figures in the history of genetics. Conveniently, their last names all begin with the letter M. Gregor Mendel, of course, is one. The second is Thomas Hunt Morgan, whose pioneering work with fruit flies provided independent confirmation of Gregor's theories. The third is Barbara McClintock.

Barbara McClintock was born in 1902 in Hartford, Connecticut. She enrolled at Cornell University and took the only undergraduate genetics course that was offered at that time. Her good showing in the class attracted the interest of Dr. Robert Hutchison, who taught a graduate course in the same subject. He invited Barbara to take his class, and that cemented her desire to learn more about genetics. She also became interested in studying chromosomes. She received her bachelor's degree in 1923 and earned a Ph.D. degree four years later.

She began doing research on the ten chromosomes that are found in maize, a type of corn that has colored kernels. During that era, there were very few women in science. At Cornell, for example, the only female professors were in the home economics department. So in addition to her research, she had to put a lot of energy into trying to find a permanent position. But she kept going. She discovered what became known as "jumping genes." That meant that genetic characteristics could "cross over," trading places on a chromosome so that brand new traits can appear. Called "recombination," it is one of the main reasons why children can look different from their parents.

Like Gregor Mendel, it took a long time for her achievements to be fully recognized. Unlike Gregor, she was still alive when that recognition occurred. She received more than two dozen honorary degrees and awards. Her highest honor came when she was awarded the Nobel Prize in Physiology or Medicine in 1983. She died in 1992.

Chronology

1822	Born on July 22 in Heinzendorf, Moravia
1833	Attends school in Leipnik
1834	Enters Imperial Royal Gymnasium in Opava
1840	Graduates from the Opava Gymnasium; enrolls at the Olmütz Philosophical Institute
1843	Enters St. Thomas monastery in Brünn and takes name of Gregor
1847	Is ordained as a priest
1849	Takes teaching job in nearby town
1850	Fails examination for teaching certificate
1851	Enrolls at the University of Vienna, focusing on natural history
1853	Returns to St. Thomas Monastery and begins research on plant heredity; publishes paper in the *Proceedings of the Natural Science Society of Brünn*
1854	Begins teaching at school in Brünn
1856	Fails examination for teaching certificate again
1862	Publishes paper on weather observations in *Austria-Hungary Natural Science Society Proceedings*
1863	Finishes research on plant heredity
1868	Elected abbot of St. Thomas monastery
1870	Elected to the Agricultural Society of Moravia
1875	Begins opposition to tax on monasteries
1884	Dies on January 6